Breakwater Rock

Other works by Bruce Lawder

Poetry

Little Choice
Shadings
Afterthoughts
Shorelines

Fiction

Dwarf Stories

Plays

Computer Time
A House in the Suburbs,
The Cherry Tree

Essays

Vers le vers

Breakwater Rock

poetry by

Bruce Lawder

Homestead Lighthouse Press
Grants Pass, Oregon

Library of Congress Cataloging-in-Publication Data Pending

Names: Bruce Lawder, author.

Library of Congress Control Number:

ISBN 978-1-950457-42-1

Homestead Lighthouse Press
110 Kitts Lane,
South Point, OH 45680
www.homesteadlighthousepress.com

Distributed by Homestead Lighthouse Press, Daedalus Distribution, Amazon.com, Barnes & Noble

Cover & Book Design: Ray Rhamey, Ashland, OR

Homestead Lighthouse Press gratefully acknowledges the generous support of its readers and patrons.

Notes and Acknowledgements

This book consists for the most part of poems written prior to and after a recent trip to the town where I grew up. It is a kind of homecoming both in time as well as in space. When I was a boy becoming aware of the etymologies of words I mistakenly thought of "exile" as "ex-île", a former island, something that I have used in "The Turning Of The Tide". The title of section IX in "Night Watch" is a partial quote from Yeats. The poems "Little Collage" and "Breakwater Rock" first appeared in *The Hudson Review.*

Contents

*Les mots survivent aux faits
qu'ils fêtent*

For Gaby

Little Collage

Pray you, draw homewards.

Once more to walk the place,
tongues in the trees,
books in the running brooks,
as if there were
no enemy
but winter and rough weather.

Exile from exile,
free at last of war –
color it blossom, color
it fall,
each leaf a letter,
silence over all.

Autumn Music

The leaves still fall
like the notes from the harp,
but the house
at the river is gone
though the water flows on.

Hardest of all
in the stricken air
is to be still
and see things clearly
the way they are.

Family Drama

Whiffleball in the yard,
drama in the rooms,
the Bible on its stand
beneath a book of rhymes –
my father's favorite role
in Shakespeare was King Lear:

the raging on the heath
or seething at the Sound
the old gnashing of teeth –
the story of the sinned
and sinned against, in several
versions, would come later.

Bullish

The clouds have made their mountains, and the lake's
no more than fields of color in the mist.
If it weren't for the white bull in the meadow,
I'd say we were in Westport once again
walking the water along the shore.
But there are no white bulls on those lawns,
not even in the best of sculpture gardens.
The bull-like shape must be that of a bull,
though you never can tell these days for sure
just where nature has ended and art begun.
At home in the mountains or up in the air –
whoever you are and wherever you are,
you are somewhere at least, both here and there.
And bullshit is bullshit, no matter where.

The Undertaker's Rebuttal

Branches are bare: there are nothing but lines
to look at here, ghost breaths of the air.
From time to time a breeze still showers down
what look like coins, though they are only
the last of the leaves from the last beech trees
falling. Forget the story. Aren't we past belief
in some sadistic, shuddering shape-shifter
staking a claim to his woman of choice
or grief? Time to get on with the work.
Leaves are leaves. Not even. Words are words.
And if they turn more brilliant as they die,
so be it. You can close your eyes. Let the leaves
flutter free for a while before they drop
and turn to compost. Grass will grow again.

Hole

I dig a hole it is nothing I lie down there and sing
I sing the hole I have made of my life it is nothing I sing
I sing the whole of the sky till it blackens and I sing the black too
I dig a hole it is nothing I lie down there and sing
I sing the star in the story and the stars on their own
I sing the night that is holy I sing the whole of the night
I dig a hole it is nothing I lie down there and sing
I sing the crow in the tree and the tree that resembles a crow
I sing of the black in the branches and the breaks in between
I dig a hole it is nothing I lie down there and sing
I sing what is written it is winter I sing what is not
I sing the black of the branch and the blank of the snow
I dig a hole it is nothing I lie down there and sing
I sing the word in the world and the world that is more than the word
I sing the black back to beginning may it root may it rise
I dig a hole it is nothing I lie down there and sing
I sing the light in the blackness and the blackness as well
I sing the hole as it darkens and the tree as it climbs to the light
I dig a hole it is nothing I lie down there and sing
I sing the word in the whole and the hole in the word
I sing what is holy I sing what is wholly my own
I dig a hole it is nothing I lie down there and sing
I sing the hole I have made of my life it is nothing I sing
I sing of the hole and am whole

Chough Talk

Take therefore no thought for the morrow.

Up into the mountains
the choughs go, over
the summits, over the snow.
Love your neighbors, they caw,
like yourself. The meek
shall inherit the earth.

Ask, ask, ask
and it shall be
given, seek, seek, seek
and it shall be found,
caw the choughs as they go
over the tree-line, over the snow.

Lamentation

I mourn
what was not mine to mourn
and I mourn what was.

I mourn
what I held in my hands
and let fall through my fingers.

I mourn
the morning as well as the night
and the nothing between.

I mourn
the light I mistook for love
and the darkness as well.

I mourn
what I fail to remember
and I mourn what I do.

I mourn
the words that died in the womb of your mouth
and the words that did not.

I mourn
what no one knows and more
I mourn the body that is ash and air.

Another Winter's Tale

The tree flies from the field and you speak of a crow.
You look at the white of the snow and say what you see.
I show you a stone from the field I have crossed.
The tree folds its wings and flies home.

You take the stone in your hand and say it is nothing.
You throw it away to the water and watch
as it sinks out of sight in the darkness.
I see how the shadows come home.

II

The Turning Of The Tide

I. Words

Once more to walk
the water, once more
to see the dark
waves peaking pour

their white-stone light
on the shelved rock,
to watch the black-
backed gulls in flight

scream, then veer off
as we approach
while the night surf
bullets the beach….

Thou shalt not kill,
said the Good Book.
Thou shalt not…. Still
take a good look

at what came round.
Could you vote
on a comet?
Could you pocket the Sound?

War, said the waves,
whore, said the star.
Nothing here saves
whatever you are.

A darkening wood,
a gingerbread house,
and the darkness ahead
as still as a mouse....

Ash, said the stone,
crumbs, said the snow.
White star blossoms alone
thread the wood that you know.

Breakwater moon,
breakwater rock,
shelter the town,
harbor the dark.

II. Hymn

O the glory of offices,
staff
and line, the genius
of the swivel chair,
the revolving door,
not to mention the grace
of moving in circles –
as long as they are
the right ones –
the ecstasy
of the elevator,
the simplicity
of the shaft,
of going up and down
in the world,
rising and falling,
day after day,
year after year!
O the long
lines of the corridors,
the song
of computers,
the architecture
of wall and window,
cubicle and cube –
the world in order,
people in their places,
pens and pencils in rows.

Look: now that you have
a window of your own
you can see for yourself
the far hills beyond
as they darken and fade
in the flood of the blue

as the world turns around
with its silences,
its inaudible sound.

III. Illuminations

We've known, of course, our own fantastic Floridas,
hotels and motels, beach parties, babed with booze,
Conquistadors of midnight, El Dorados built of sand,
the mud of ghettoes, garbage, rivers choked

with bodies, chained and noosed, the town parade
of hoods, and, in the street, a squad car, waiting.
O rage to order, "blessèd rage", as the poet once said,
the black hull filled with white moonlight.

IV. Drought

Now that the summer of our discontent
has dried up everything, now that the earth
has lost its rags of color, and the ground

has been burnt back to something bleaker,
blacker, now that the trees no longer break
in the first wind, but wither at the root,

now that the fall has fallen, and the branches
have shed their voices and the vaulted stars,
now that the green and gold mosaics

we trod on have begun to blacken
beneath our steps, can we, too, not begin
to welcome in the winter and accept

the erasure of almost everything? Already
a snow is sifting in from the margins, shifting
a blankness onto the branches, brightening

the architecture. Soon even the bare, ruined choirs
will crumble, and what we called the ground beneath our feet
vanish until there is nothing to walk on but words.

V. Another Face

O the beauty of mountains,
the beauty of a face,
another face,
in shadow or in light,
the slow ascent
and danger
hold on hold….

Isn't love something
like this, climbing
together, bound
each to the other,
fault
on fault, one
still and the other
moving, one moving
and the other
still, each
belaying the other,
crossing
fissure and fold,
this breath
rope,
mounting
higher and higher,
distance
to distance,
fleck, edge
and ledge, together,
extending the pleasure,
until,
at the peak,
what you have worked for,
the summit, vanishes,
and suddenly
now here there is
nowhere to go….

VI. Lullaby

Quiet!
Don't wake the poet.
Walt Whitman lies
in the buffalo grass,

wrapped in the stray
lines of another day
behind the used-car lot
at the end of the road.

VII. The Sound

It was
only the Sound,
alone,
you heard, at night,
walking the water,

dodging the dull
relentless firing line
of the surf
as the words in waves
kept repeating themselves:

to kill, or
not to kill,
that
is the question,
as later

to love,
or not to love,
and what
among the lies
and fictions to believe….

See: the egret
where the tide
goes out,
a night
light in the dark.

VIII. For The Birds

To be
as the tree
is, rooted in the earth,
even if only
in the dark
of the mind,
to rise
by rooting, to know
the down-
ward, dark-
ward, dirt-
ward
plunge to the light,
to see
how you have made
a place
not only for yourself
but for the birds,
seeding the word
crumbs,
and not only a song,
a sheltering
shade.

IX. Envoi

Stars,
the white
stones,

blossoming,
out of
the waves,

the dark
pit
and peak….

Egret,
you night
lamp,

exile,
your former island,
lets you go.

Origins

Trace your ancestry all the way back to Adam and Eve, the primal family, and, if you are honest, you will have to encounter the problematics not only of patriarchy, in your quest for innocence, but of incest as well, and thus, in your desire for something like the primary, if not the primitive, place of paradise, if that is what you really want, to discover another source of original sin: not in the Tree of Knowledge but the Tree of Life. Would it not be healthier, and for each and every one of us, to place our origins in the Big Bang, not in the small one, and to see ourselves and all our ancestors, equally, as descendants of dust? Stardust, of course. From stardust to stardust, that is the motto, especially for those of us who in our lives have always tried to follow our own star. So let it be written.

Piece Of Fruit

You want another story and so you walk out into the orchard at the foot of the wood and pick one. The wood is a dark wood, and not because a writer once said so but because of itself: it grows in its own shadow, like the fruit tree, and it needs the shading leaves to transform the light so that with its increasing strength it can go down deeper into the dirt and darkness to stand up even taller to the day and night. Once the rest of the fruit falls, once the fall itself fades, there will be nothing left of the leaves to help you recognize the identity of the tree but its bark and shape. And the story that you hold in your hands, this particular piece of fruit? It is your story now: taste and see.

Witnesses

We can not believe for long that the terrible things of this world not only actually happen, but keep on happening, and when we read of them it is as if we were reading not something from our time, not even something from the shelves of history, but some kind of allegory we have yet to understand. Who among us would ever think of walking into a town or village, for example, only to call the people out into the public square to murder them? On what authority? Who is responsible for the order not to cry? Whoever cries will be shot, as if mourning itself had become a crime. Let the children be separated, someone says, so that the parents can watch them dig the graves. But it will not be the children who are shot. It will be the parents, and in front of the children, who, should anyone cry out, will all be shot themselves. Those are the orders. They will be followed. This is not a fiction. There are witnesses, there must be witnesses, it would seem, though who should bear witness for the witnesses is another question, and one no one, at least for the moment, is asking.

In Praise Of Diversity

Many a person would like his or her existence to be structured in or through some form of idea or belief, even what an early American philosopher and a later poet once called "the central idea", though in our contrary and contradictory time it might be only the absence of such a form that we discover at the heart of things. Imagine for one moment each and every one of us as a voice in a chorus and the chorus you imagine will inevitably be as diverse as its members, at least when we are not singing according to script or score. Is that not true, as far as the logic goes? But what of the multiple voices within us, the interior music, so to speak, not only of the serial but of the simultaneous selves we want to sing and celebrate, if not the absences that we assume, and, from time to time, mourn and lament? Are not these voices equally valid as voices even in the void and not invalid vices to be shunned? Is not each and every one of us a diversity unto herself or himself, a multitude not only of voices but of silences as well? Put down your book or pencil, step outside, look in to the world with your ears or listen with your eyes. See: even in a single tree, ash or oak, whatever the word, how many songs, how many silences!

In The Absence Of Heroes

One does not want the story or the poem to have a hero, and certainly not oneself, even if it is only our own story we are talking about, the only story we can ever hope to know, and not only because no one is more aware of our weaknesses and failings than we ourselves, but because a story with a hero is hardly ever a happy one, and in this democratic age, democratic in theory at least, no one should stand out, no one should be less, or more, than equal. As to the stories, what we know with certainty is that we will not have the last word, and what is true of the future is also true of the past. Look far enough into the light or dark before or behind you and what you will see, if you see any-thing, are holes, black holes. The Tree of Ignorance, not Knowledge, grows beside the Tree of Life.

Dark Light

You are walking along the beach at night, even if it is only what you hold in your mind now, the night you carry with you still wherever you go, picking your way across the stones and abandoned shells, looking at the moon that somehow still resembles your young self, lop-sided and in need of a shave. If the surface of the sea is a mirror, it is a mirror you can dive into, dissolving it and yourself in a dark and depth you cannot otherwise feel or fathom. For there really is another world out there, an underwater world of danger, a world of reefs and rocks and even wrecks still beautiful in the blue and fluent light. Who has taken the plunge who does not remember something of that first night swim as the waves continue to rattle overhead like a rain of bullets while in your hands another space takes shape, finite and infinite at once? Was it not like what making love would be, that immersion in the chill salt and phosphorescent dark, and even if in time it would become as ordinary or as natural as the stretch marks on a woman's hips, it was and is a world unto itself, the milky way you swam and still swim in, the stars themselves: deep darknesses, heavenly stairs.

The Sound

It is not really the sea you see, you tell yourself, it is the Sound, the water trapped and flowing in between an island and a continent, and what you hear, if it is the sound of the sea, must be the sea in miniature, as the waves break once more, blossoming and retreating, like flowers, returning to the depths, the silences, from which they have come. Earlier, standing at the edge of the harbor, looking out into the distance at the white-caps, it was the going out you saw, as, now, it is the coming in. After all, this is where the women of the family are buried, though buried is hardly the word for a scattering of ashes, but enough to make of the white-caps something more than waves. See: once again they rise, if only in thought, the unburied, mother and sisters, and the Sound resounds in the silence, as it always has, time and again, with no end in sight.

Approaching Winter

The snow will soon be upon us, the bright eraser, the blank that blankets almost everything. Already the leaves have fallen, the simmering glory of color has come and gone in the trees, as has our earlier summering in the shade, and now in the distance before us there are only the bare lines of the branches, blacker and bleaker each day, though when we walk the woods the fallen leaves still retain something of ancient Ravenna in the green and gold mosaics beneath our feet. Walk far enough, walk the year round, or almost round, and you will come again upon the chapel that you love, the imagined one, with its leaves of real light, each pane, unstoried now, unstained, and practically unsung.

Beyond The Words

We cannot find the words to say what it is in the world that we love, or why we love what we do – alas! Or so we say. Yet why bemoan the situation? Should we not celebrate, should we not glory in the fact that language inevitably comes up short, that there is something fundamental beyond ourselves in the world, something real and wonderful, something to reach for, something in the silence itself? Something, in other words, beyond the words.

A Salt Language

The bittern my bird flies free of the marshes, free of the salt, the ooze, the bitterness of reeds; and I see, once again, in the wingwhir and silence of a flight, a suggestion, in movement, of the essential: the thing itself, the word, *ousa*, essence and existence, presence and absence at once.

IV

Night Watch

I. Local Color

Hand-dug sand holes,
clams in sea-weed,
sea-weed in sand
covered with coals –

a local picnic,
mothers and fathers,
children and neighbors,
whole families, iconic,

as each boat in the harbor
of the darkening Sound
turns on its anchor
buried underground

and one of the futures
shreds a paper sky,
reversing the mirrors:
time to live, time to die….

You know something is wrong
when you have to put
a gun or a foot
on the throat of your song.

II. Rhythm And Rhyme

O the joy
of rhythm and rhyme
in a darkening time,
love it
or leave it,
better dead
than red,
search and destroy.

O the psalm
of Agent Orange
and napalm,
the bombs
bursting in air
like words,
blasphemous
balm.

III. Longer Lines

Let us now praise the longer lines at Macy's,
the objects on the shelf at the local A & P,
the promised paradise of window shoppers,
combinations of color, inhuman harmony!

But try to vote or even buy a beer….
What could you do but count the body bags
of garbage at your feet while waiting for
the call to kill amid the rags and flags?

IV. Fall

The light
has gone out
of the leaves.
They hang like letters
from the tree,
withering.

Who will
bury the body
for the spirit to rest?
Who will breathe
new life
into the shade?

V. Silences

Was it you,
was it really you,
and no one but you
standing there
alone in the light
and your back
to the water,
admiring
the view and the house
I could never give you,
the one
with nothing
in the rooms
and the columns of air?

VI. At The Sound

O the beauty of buttocks and breasts,
dark couplings in the sands,
the run and reach of flesh,
the bogged-down, slogged swamp sounds.

What's tomorrow for you?
It's always night
when whatever you do
nothing is right.

VII. Pearls

To pick at the shells,
examine the driftwood,
wade into the water
and watch the gulls,

the screaming sea-birds,
fly off with the omens
as if they were words,
then try your amens.

Love it or leave it,
better dead than red.
Hard to believe it,
but that's what was said.

Paper, screamed the gull,
shreds, cried the sky:
if you don't want to kill,
you must learn how to die.

Ash, said the snow,
grains of sand, said the sea,
stones in a row –
from here to eternity.

Breakwater moon,
breakwater rock,
shelter the country,
harbor the dark.

VIII. Voice In The Chorus

O the song
of the shrouds
ghosting the harbor,
chains
rattling the air,
boats
hosting a voyage
still
not there….

Sing, then,
you, too, sing,
in the silence,
the absence,
sing to celebrate
the other
and at the same
time mourn
the living and the lost,
the dying, the unborn,
as if
what you had been
but are no longer,
and what
you would become,
could be
part of the one
arc,
part of the one
journey, the story
traced in the dark….

See: even in the late
light of the stones,
the peaks
still spread their blanks,
their buds, their blossoms,
billowing sails.

IX. All Hands Are Lunatic

To read
by the light

of the moon,

to be
borne again

on the salt

waste and wake
of the water,

to look

at the starred
dark of our time

and find

what you can
walk on,

words.

At The Sea

The gathered clouds disintegrate
into the crystals of a snow
that we watch yielding at the sea –
that restless beautiful black world
they cannot enter as they are

but at that salt heat are transformed
into a darker, warmer shower:
dapple and dazzle of the day
that shadows like a pencil sketch
the rain of these abandoned moments.

c. 1971

Crossing The Waters

*Thus in the beginning all
the world was America....*

White as spilt milk, the ice
we can see in the waters
off Greenland, flying back
to New York, repeating the arc
of the epic ancestors.

They stripped their names at the border,
the immigration police,
and gave them the one I must carry
forever, as if it were mine,
even in the other direction.

Breakwater Rock

Still harbor, still the ground,
a scattering like ash
of snow, a sowing, as
in frozen furrows seed
fresh-flung to anchor
the silence of the Sound….

Always the women's place,
this water, cold and dark,
the old breakwater rock
the arms of an embrace
open to absence,
to all time and space.

Winter In Westport

A salt
tide still rides
the river,
bringing home
the sea-trout.
But childhood
sinks like mud
now, hardening
under its own weight,
or else
goes up in air,
a puddle after rain.

Still
something remains
in the bed at low tide,
even if it is
no more
than this driftwood
or a bicycle wheel
in earth
too treacherous
for us to use
or excavate, this
inhospitable humus.

Out
in the harbor
the coldest of winters
has frozen the salt
waves
of the Sound
into a silence,
the darkness
visible at last,
an ice
lace
veils the ground….

Even this late
I'm drawn to the place,
haunting the old
seedtime, as if
in a flicker of light
or a flick of the wrist
I could
still
sow the ash
of snow
into these, the darkest
of furrows.

Surge

A dance
of birches
in the woods,

the sycamore
a woman's
fate, the future,

and over all
the rising
and the fall

an old gnarled elm
still steadfast, steadying
the helm….

Gone now
the woods, the water,
but I still can see

through clouds
the harp of sunlight
in your hands.

Stained Glass

Mud,
crushed shells,
sand,

borne
free of the salt,
the sea,

fired
to liquid
light,

dyed,
then cooled
to color,

cut,
and pieced
together,

the paned,
the stained
story.

The Sweet And The Salt

Lakes
are islands,
the mountains
flow downwards,
depositing
their rocks,
their burdens,
bringing
their rage
of water
to the shore.

But the sea
is in us, in our own
dark passages,
a salt
rush, tow
and undertow,
in the in-
finite, slow
erasures,
the lost
horizons.

See:
here, too,
is the forest of masts,
the cormorant's
sign of the cross,
the slate
slabs
cut from the mountain
roofing the marshland
we walk on, our un-
written memorials.

Look: in the distance,
the ice
fields billow again,
summit on summit,
and the salt seeds
blossom once more
beyond the summer
as the light's
blown back
against the black,
a further flowering.

Figura

Neither in-
side nor out,

but in
between,

the leaf
life left

to window,
storied, un-

storied, starred
and stained:

the imagined
chapel,

the actual
light.

A Note About the Author

Bruce Lawder grew up in Westport, Connecticut and now divides his time with his wife, the painter Gabrielle Lawder-Ruedin, between Switzerland and France. In addition to writing poems, stories and plays, he has also published critical articles on poetry and painting in the United States, France, Germany, Austria and Switzerland. He has a B.A. in English and American Literature from Dartmouth College and a Ph.D. in Comparative Literature from the University of Zurich. Before deciding to earn his living as a teacher, he was an actor at the Charles Street Playhouse in Boston, Massachusetts. He has published four volumes of poetry as well as a book of short fiction, *Dwarf Stories,* and a collection of essays on poetic structure, *Vers le vers.* Three of his plays, *Computer Time, A House in the Suburbs,* and *The Cherry Tree,* were recently performed by the American Theatre of Actors in New York City, with a fourth, *Traitors,* scheduled for production later this year.